The Love of Ponies

The Love of Ponies

ANNE ALCOCK

OCTOPUS

Contents

First published 1975 by Octopus Books Limited
59 Grosvenor Street, London W1

ISBN 0 7064 0454 8

© 1975 Octopus Books Limited

Distributed in USA by Crescent Books
a division of Crown Publishers Inc
419 Park Avenue South
New York, N.Y. 10016

Produced by Mandarin Publishers Limited
Westlands Road, Quarry Bay, Hong Kong

Printed in Hong Kong

Native Breeds

Many children who own a Welsh Mountain pony will instantly recognize this as one [*right*] by its wide forehead, big, kind eyes, pricked ears and deep, broad chest. Yet few of them will have seen it in its native countryside, as fewer visitors reach the Brecon Mountains than, for instance, the New Forest.

One of the most intelligent of breeds, the Welsh Mountain pony is also, without doubt, exceptionally beautiful and as such is a great favourite. Combined with its almost Arab-like head, high tail carriage and gay action, it is also a successful show pony.

The Welsh Mountain pony has lived in countryside like this [*left*] literally since before history; his hardiness and intelligence having helped him survive through the ages.

Welsh Mountain ponies, which are only 12 hands high or less, are great fun to ride and always willing. They will even carry adults, in spite of their tiny size. They frequently do so in Wales when the farmer rides them to shepherd his sheep or harnesses them to a trap which they pull with equal vigour. From them the larger Welsh pony has developed, ideal as a child's second pony, and it is also said that the Welsh Mountain pony has contributed towards producing the polo pony, hunter, hackney, Welsh Cob and possibly, in the earliest stage of its development, the thoroughbred. Certainly he has some of the refined qualities which go to make up the thoroughbred.

The breed society for Welsh ponies and cobs has four sections, A for the Welsh Mountain pony, B for the Welsh Pony, C the Welsh pony of Cob Type, and D, the biggest of them, the Welsh Cob.

The last three all derive from the ancient Welsh Mountain pony and inherit much of its attributes, such as their soundness, tough constitutions, and ability to carry weight.

They are also excellent jumpers and indeed make ideal all-round family ponies, excelling at gymkhana games, successful at showing and jumping, and no day is too long for them out hunting.

I well remember the fun I had learning to ride on a riding school's Welsh Mountain pony, winning my first rosette on her, and enjoying a wonderful introduction to hunting from her back.

A familiar scene by the roadside to the thousands of visitors who swarm to England's New Forest every summer are these mares and foals. Roaming in their natural habitat, the mares usually produce a foal each spring. The best survive to ensure the sound future of the breed and, as for the other native breeds, that means picking what they can out of rough, coarse grass and heathland.

Cars have created a problem for the New Forest pony because many ponies have been tempted to the roadside having learnt to associate cars with titbits, only to be killed by other vehicles tearing through. Now signs throughout the forest—the Royal hunting grounds of ancient English kings and known as the 'New Forest' since King William Rufus 900 years ago—warn against feeding the ponies. In addition, more fences and ditches have been built in an effort to keep them off the roads but sadly, each year, some of the 2,000 ponies roaming the 60,000-acre forest are still killed.

On the other hand, ponies taken off the moor and broken-in have proved to be good in traffic, an invaluable asset these days! Since they see more people when roaming free than other native breeds do, they are often easier to break in, and as they range from 12 h.h. to 14 h.h. they can suit most members of the family. Here [*above right*] some wild ones have already made friends with families, enjoying a holiday paddle with some children.

Much of the New Forest, in Hampshire in southern England, is heathland and all that remains of the formerly heavily-timbered forest are outcrops of conifers and oaks. A favourite type of picknicking place with visitors is a glade like this [*below left*] showing off the beauty of Britain with the sun filtering through the oaks and shining on the silver birch, while the movement of a solitary pony rustles the fallen leaves. The grass is short, almost as if it were a mown lawn, from the constant grazing of it by ponies. The golden light [*above left*] illustrates the beauty of autumn as the ponies and foals pick their way through the hummocks. The poor quality of food available to him has made the New Forest pony an economical feeder, which is reflected in the cost of keeping him when he has been sold and broken-in as a riding pony. Like the other native breeds, they are used to picking their way across rough ground and this has made them sure-footed with a good, fairly high action. Although their hindquarters are narrower than some other native ponies they have depth through the heart and good, strong shoulders so that they, too, are capable of carrying adults. The constant struggle for survival by native breeds has developed in them intelligence, resolution and guile, but it has not made them bad tempered, quite the reverse in fact, as they are docile, friendly and willing to do what the rider wants.

The New Forest pony has become a less pure native breed because of the introduction, at about the turn of the century, of 'foreign' stallions from other British breeds and even some Arab stallions who were turned loose. Bringing the high-class blood of the latter into the forest and expecting it to be able to cope with the harsh life and poor conditions was doomed to failure but even though it did not last long the New Forest pony varies more and is less true to type because of it. This situation is not likely to last indefinitely, because stallions are now inspected every year and if any are not considered good enough they are not allowed to remain. This pony also has been popular with buyers from America, Canada, Holland, Denmark and other countries.

The best known and most popular of all the native breeds is the diminutive, totally loveable and mischievous Shetland pony, a real character who has been responsible for giving countless numbers of children confidence in horses. As the smallest breed (his height is often measured in inches instead of hands) his size does not frighten even the smallest toddlers and he can be guaranteed to give a whole generation loads of fun, with a twinkle in his large, kindly eyes, and with his gay, sprightly action. He can have quite a mind of his own and ponies as a whole do tend to be naughtier than horses. Shetlands live to a great age, nearly always remaining sound and well, thus they are often able to teach the next generation. Because they look so cuddly, Shetland ponies are sometimes kept as pets and can be seen grazing on lawns, so dispensing with the need for a lawn mower! I have even heard of one allowed in the house like a dog!

But life was not always so easy for the Shetland. Before ponies became so popular for riding and before the modernization of industry, the Shetland pony lived a hard life in the mines, toiling to bring loads of coal to the surface. They were used because their tiny size meant they were able to walk along the low, narrow tunnels but their health suffered in the dust and the bright light hurt their eyes when they were brought back to the surface.

It was harder, even, than the wild life in their native Shetland Isles where they withstood the toughest elements nature could provide, survived and even thrived on it. It was thought that it was their stark existence which had made them so small but Shetlands have been produced in the south for many years now and their size has not changed. Food can become so sparse during the freezing winter in the islands that the ponies pick their way down to the coast [*above*] to eat seaweed. Funnily enough a seaweed extract is now used for high-class animals like racehorses to bring out a shine in their coat. Although their coat is shaggy and very thick in the winter [*above right*] to guard against the cold, the Shetland has a fine, glossy summer coat, an illustration of his health.

Before a parent is tempted to rush off and buy one of these adorable animals he must bear in mind the time needed to care for him: if the pony is turned out in a field to live he must be checked every day even when the children are at school, to see that he has not cut himself, that he has water and in winter, some hay. His feet should be tended to by a blacksmith and not allowed to grow too long or they will be painful. In return he will reward the family with hours of pleasure.

Just compare the refined head of an American Shetland pony [*right*] to the woolly one of the native British example. The

American version of the Shetland pony has developed this almost thoroughbred-Arabian look through selective breeding and the best examples fetch fabulous sums of money. The pony has, however, retained its sturdiness, and a height limit of 46 inches set by the American Shetland Pony Club has ensured that it retains its best known characteristic, its small size. Indeed, tiny American Shetland ponies of only about 28 inches are very popular in that country. The almost delicate look about the pony with its dainty ears, slightly dished face, arched neck and sleek coat hides the fact that it is still basically the hardy product of the Shetland Isles, and in spite of the high prices paid for many of them it is still possible to buy one as a pet. They are bred in a wide range of colours, too.

The American Shetland pony has been a great favourite in the American show-ring, where they sometimes jump a low course, showing off their paces, wearing weighted shoes which make them prance extravagantly, and with their tails, which have been set, held high. They are also popular under Western saddle or in harness, when they can pull a child's gig or make a colourful display in a team. In harness classes their style and manners come to the fore and in pony-roadster classes they step out briskly. Now they have become even more popular for trotting racing, pulling little sulkies and giving loads of excitement to their young drivers.

Rugged and wild, like the area it lives in, the Dartmoor pony throws up its head as a human approaches [*below*]. All the nine native breeds of Great Britain are hardy and tough, but there the similarity ends. Each breed has developed and adapted to its different tracts of land; for the Dartmoor this means a vast moorland topped by granite tors mostly over 1,000 feet high. The bleak and windswept slopes falling away from the tors have been grazed by the little Dartmoor pony since time immemorial. The country is of little use and is best known for its tourists and for a prison whose tight security net a convict would find very hard to elude. Even having done so, it would be difficult for him to survive on the cold, misty moor with its treacherous bogs.

The best of the Dartmoor breed survives in spite of the grim and forbidding surroundings. One feels a certain awe in looking at the great rocky tors and bleak expanses, but to live on it would make many a visitor shudder. For the tourists there is an easy way out: the car enables them to look at the imposing surroundings in comfort. Some of the ponies have become wise to the fact that a car can mean titbits, so drivers should never travel fast in case they round a bend to find some ponies in their path.
Few of the mares and even fewer of the stallions are ever handled except for branding, but the breed has earned itself a fine name as riding ponies from the stock taken off the moor and broken-in. If this is done when they are young enough and still tractable they make excellent riding ponies, and their high head carriage gives a child a good feel. Compact, with small pricked ears, strong quarters, and full tail, the Dartmoor pony is also extremely long-lived and loves children, which makes it ideal for a whole family to grow up on. He is strong enough, too, to carry an adult and will safely take one hunting in his native area.
At one time the breed was in some danger, because the local people, wanting an even smaller pony to work in the

mines, introduced some Shetlands and a poor quality cross-breed was allowed to roam on the moor. They also suffered in the Second World War when Dartmoor ponies were used for training troops. Luckily the Dartmoor Pony Society and some individual breeders stepped in to preserve the true breed and they can now be found in America and Canada as well as several European countries.

The strongest and usually the largest native breed of Britain is Scotland's Highland pony. Thick-set and powerfully-built, he is capable of carrying or pulling enormous weights. Set in the magnificent Highlands of Scotland, the Highland pony has long been the friend of the few inhabitants there, carrying round his land the crofter who largely survives on subsistence farming, miles away from towns and railways. The pony provides transport for the deer-stalker and is useful on the hills, being sure-footed and a good walker. He is to be found, too, on some of the islands off the coast, where he is usually smaller. Both types are no longer clean-bred, some Arab and other blood having been infused at the end of the last century. These contented-looking ponies [*right*] are grazing on the Isle of Rhum, and many are also found on the Isles of Barra and Mull off the west coast of Scotland.
The Highland ponies have great character, yet in spite of their appearance they are in no way sluggish. They also possess very fine hair, a soft, velvety muzzle and long manes and tails. As a riding pony they are popular and as successful as most.
The Highland pony probably evolved after the Ice Age when the larger ponies drifted to the north to what is now Scotland and Scandinavia, while the smaller ponies settled southwards.

The mealy-muzzled Exmoor is one of my favourite pony characters and here [*right*] is a group of mares and foals on their native moor which stretches between Devon and Somerset.
The pony is one of the oldest native breeds, its history being lost in antiquity; it probably stems from the original British wild horse. Life on the moor has made it tough, strong and sure-footed. When broken-in for riding it has a good, high action as a result of having picked up its feet carefully over stones and rough ground in early life. It can be bleak and bitterly cold in winter on the moor thus the pony grows a thick, matted coat but in the summer a gloss comes out in it. The Exmoor pony is useful to farmers on the moor and besides carrying them around their land the ponies willingly take adults hunting all day. It is a tremendous sign of his strength and stamina that he can carry a man all day and still be able to keep pace with horses—and probably does better than them because of his ability to cope with the moorland! There are many hunts on the moor, both Foxhounds and Staghounds, and very few 'antis' make their voices heard down there. Apart from its distinctive mealy nose, the same oatmeal colouring is found inside the ear and sometimes under the stomach. There is never any white anywhere. They are small ponies but very sound, their breed society stipulating 12.2 h.h. as the maximum for mares and 12.3 h.h. for stallions. The body has great depth and width to make up for lack of height enabling them to carry big weights.

[*left*] One breed whose origin is known for certain is the Morgan, which stems from one little stallion in America and has a remarkable story. In the 1790s, after a chequered start to life in Vermont, a certain smart, small horse, that was probably partly Arabian or Thoroughbred, was given to an inn-keeper by the name of Thomas Justin Morgan living in Massachusetts, in payment of a debt. The horse had no name and became known simply as Justin Morgan's horse. He was a bay with black points and white star and he stood 14 h.h. No-one could have expected anything extraordinary from him as he went about his work pulling a cart. True, he won several weight-pulling contests and races for his owner who, liking to make a bit of extra money on the side, let him cover some mares for a fee. This was where the phenomenon came in, for no matter what sort of mare mated, whether good, poor, big or small, the progeny all looked like the father. Soon his fame spread and the U.S. army established the Morgan Stud Farm. Even now the same characteristics have been passed on, as can be seen from this fine bay colt foal with its black markings. The breed is one of the best for all-round purposes in America.

[*above right*] In the lovely Connemara district of the west of Ireland overlooking beautiful Galway Bay are found some of the oldest native ponies of all, the Connemara. Bigger than some native breeds, his height limit is 14.2 h.h. and as such makes an ideal second pony, especially as stamina is one of his best known attributes. No day out hunting is too long for him, and he gets plenty of the best of that sport in his native country. He is also an excellent jumper and makes an ideal Pony Club performer. He was left in his wild moorland state for longer than most other British breeds but is now much in demand for riding. His ancestry is lost in time, the idea that he stemmed from Spanish Armada horses which were

shipwrecked off the coast of Ireland certainly being a fallacy. It is quite possible, though, that Spanish stallions influenced the breed when the two countries traded but it is thought far more likely that the original Connemara, along with Highland, Shetland, Iceland and Norwegian ponies, stemmed from the wild horse of Mongolia, making a Celtic type pony across that part of Europe after they were split up by the Ice Age. Since then a certain amount of Arab blood has added a little refinement and the ponies have a good head and action. My family once had one who was a great all-round performer; he won Chase-me-Charlie jumping competitions and many others, yet remained a quiet character.

There are large numbers of grey Connemara ponies. Here are two of them in their wild state in Galway.

One of the loveliest beauty spots in England is the Lake District in the north-west, with its magnificent peaks towering over beautiful lakes, and its native pony, the Fell. This is another pony which has found life a little easier during this century. As the Shetlands worked underground in the mines, so the Fells carried lead from the mines to the docks in the north of England. These ponies, almost always dark in colour and about 13.2 h.h., were sent on these journeys in droves, a most unusual method. One man would be mounted and he drove the rest, much like a flock of sheep, and instead of pulling carts loaded with the lead, when a driver would have been needed for each pony, the lead was distributed in baskets on either side of the ponies' sides, each basket probably carrying eight stone. They were driven at a steady walk but nevertheless they generally covered 240 miles every week. The Fell pony's neighbour across the Pennine Ridge to the east is the slightly larger and stockier, but also dark-coloured, Dale pony. They, too, were used for this work.

The Fell pony is now a popular riding pony and since a section for the breed was opened in the National Pony Society stud book at the turn of the century, the breed has improved making a fine dual-purpose animal, for riding and driving.

Much the same can be said of the Dale pony, which is generally recognized as the largest and heaviest of the British native breeds. The picture [*above*] shows what a good-looking, albeit workmanlike, pony he is, with his thick, curly mane, tail and heel feathers, neat and alert head, strong back and quarters and kind, bright eye.

Like the Fell pony, he is an exceptional trotter and in the old days they used to compete in trotting races. They were very popular ponies being able to pull a ton in weight, or carry a farmer safely around the steep slopes of his farm, but the Dale pony was seriously threatened by the advent of cars and tractors and mechanization at the mines. Here, again, just one or two faithful breeders kept them going and today they are much appreciated as all-round ponies.

[*below and right*] Even if Iceland is not always covered in snow this is an appropriate scene with which to associate an Icelandic pony! This tough breed was actually the only form of transport in Iceland for 1000 years. Indeed, they have played a fascinating part in the country's history ever since two Norwegians, by the name of Ingolf and Leif, fed up with their king, Harold Fairhair, settled in Iceland in A.D. 870. They brought with them their families, all their household belongings—and their ponies. They were joined by others from their country and from Ireland and Scotland, with which countries they traded. As a result, the Iceland breed has developed since that time from a mixture of the ponies of those places.

In less civilized times the Icelandic people thought nothing of using their ponies for a type of fighting, much like cock-fighting, and they ate their horseflesh, too.

It was common practice, right until motorized transport came in, to turn the ponies loose at the end of a long journey to find their own way home, a task they did unerringly, like a homing pigeon! The pony has remained true to its type throughout the thousand years (an attempt to inject thoroughbred blood failed) and the unusual characteristic of this tough, rugged pony is its action, which more closely resembles an amble or shuffle than anything else. They are usually between 12 h.h. and 13 h.h., often grey, good between the shafts (they were imported by the English as pit ponies) and for riding, and they are virtually without vices—a case of handsome is what handsome does!

[*left*] The Fjord pony of Norway is nearly always dun coloured with a black dorsal stripe which runs along the back and right up the neck to the forelock. To show off this unusual characteristic, the mane is usually clipped to about four or five inches so that it stands up in a crest, clear of the black stripe. They are stocky, compact, rather heavy ponies of 14 h.h. to 14.2 h.h. which probably also stem from the Celtic type of pony, and are typically tough, docile and hard-working. In fact, the Fjord pony is friendly and fond of company. Although he is inclined to have a will of his own, he is also tireless, and is often used for draught work. His uses have diminished with the advent of the tractor, however he is still invaluable on the steep slopes of Norway. When they are hauling timber or doing other heavy work they will be given oats, otherwise they live off hay in the winter, housed communally with cattle, pigs and other livestock, and in the summer they are often tethered out at grass.

[*below left*] There are some 40 different breeds found in Russia where State Studs ensure their future. In such a vast country breeds have developed different characteristics to suit the various geographic and climatic areas. This Viatka pony [*below left*] hails from the basins of the Viatka and Obva rivers and is a typical example: dun coloured with a black dorsal stripe (they are also grey or roan), thick-set and strong, with short legs, a deep chest, well-sprung ribs and fairly small head. To combat the intense cold they not only grow a thick winter coat, but also form an extra layer of fat for more protection. Usually standing between 13 h.h. and 14 h.h., the pony is adept at pulling Troika sledges over the snow. Their unusual trotting gait is suitable for the snowbound routes, as well as giving remarkable speed.

[*top right*] One of my greatest delights in visiting the scenic country of Austria is seeing the beautiful Haflinger ponies. Easily recognizable by their rich chestnut colour and long, flowing cream

manes and tails, in summer they can
be seen either pulling in loads of
hay, when the grass is dried on rails
or round a pole, or hauling the timber
logs from the sweet-smelling pine forests,
and in winter merrily tripping over the
snow in studded shoes pulling a
sleigh, their harness bells ringing gaily
and their flaxen manes adding to
the prettiness.

When they are not working the
Haflingers are often turned out in
mountain pastures; a crisp, clear stream
spouting downwards nearby, the
bracing air penetrating their lungs. They
are seen all over Austria, but especially
in the Tyrol and Bavaria, where
they mingle with the wild flowers such
as blue gentian and edelweiss, the
little white, star-like flower which is
Austria's national emblem and from
which the Haflinger's brand mark—the
flower with the letter H in the centre—is
designed.

The Haflinger pony is strong and
sure-footed and not afraid of hard work
which has made him a popular import to
many other countries. Although it is
not known for sure how they evolved,
modern Haflingers descend from a
half-bred Arab. They are renowned for
longevity, often working for 40 years!

[*right*] Always a favourite because of its
striking colour, the Appaloosa is also a
very good riding horse. A certain
amount of Arab bred into it has
resulted in a pony or horse of between
about 14.2 h.h. and 15.2 h.h. with a
refined head and gay action. It was
produced in America by the Nez Perce
Indians of the Palouse country of
Central Idaho. When this Red Indian
tribe was completely wiped out by the
U.S. army in a battle in 1877 the breed
luckily survived. It had been used by
the Indians mainly for war but it soon
became a favourite with the circus, for
parades, and as a riding horse. It is
possible that the breed, or something
akin to it, was found in China some 3,000
years ago, because paintings of that
time depict spotted horses. They have a
pink skin under the white hair and the
spots of black or chocolate can actually
be felt superimposed on the skin.

19

Ponies for Fun

[*left*] What nicer way of cooling off on a hot summer's day
is there than to trot down to the beach and wade in? With a
group of friends it is even more fun. This group at
Putsborough, Devon, has the added advantage of a beautiful
backcloth of the majestic coastline.
The sea water cools off the ponies' legs and keeps at bay the
wretched flies that so often accompany them in the heat.
Besides being refreshing, salt water is also beneficial to legs
and can help reduce swelling and pain in a case of injury.
The ponies join in the children's fun pawing at the water
and splashing each other or jumping over the little waves.

[*above*] Let's get rid of the itches of the day! A good bit of
back-scratching does one a power of good! Some ponies roll
more than others. My first pony used to roll religiously
within seconds of being turned out in his paddock after a
ride. It used to be great fun watching him paw the
ground, sniff it (just to make sure the selected spot was

suitable, no doubt!) then get down and roll this way and
that, struggling to roll from one side to the other, which is not
easy with a rigid backbone in between. Then he would
get up and shake himself and repeat the process, usually
several times more. You should brush out the sweat in a pony
before turning him loose, but even so some ponies find there
is no substitute for a roll.
Rolling in a stable can be a problem because of the risk of the
pony getting cast, that is, stuck in the corner and unable to
extricate himself. To prevent this you should see that the
stable is not too small and that its sides are well banked up
with bedding, which will also act against draughts blowing
onto the pony's legs. Often, when a stable pony is turned
loose in a field for the first time in weeks or months, he
does not know what to do first: buck, gallop, munch the
sweet grass or have a good roll—usually in the muddiest
patch! Some ponies save up everything for this occasion and
seldom or never roll in a box.

show class it is some consolation to know that his agility will earn him rosettes in the gymkhana ring. The essence of these games is fun, for there is a lot of evidence to show that it is fun for the pony, too. A really good gymkhana pony soon learns to stop the moment the music does in musical chairs, and to recognize that a line of poles is for nipping in and out of in a bending race! Here a flag race is in progress [*left*]. There is no end of permutations for gymkhana games, some even having two riders gallop bareback on one pony! The introduction of the Prince Philip Cup Mounted Games has fulfilled its intention of giving the ordinary ponies a chance to do well when they have no chance in other forms of competition. The final at the Horse of the Year Show at Wembley is one of the highlights of each evening, the crowds roar support for 'their' teams, making the atmosphere as tense and electrifying, if a little more light-hearted, as any jump-off for a major show-jumping competition.

[*above*] Having had an introduction to gymkhana events that were not over ambitious, a child is soon ready to have a go alone. There is a sense of achievement in inducing your pony to do that much better than your friends'. To do so you will have had him obeying your commands, which had to be quick and snappy because every second counted. And if you have a pony that will always stand at the bottom of a

[*below*] Who is this more fun for, the rider, the pony or the runner? I'll take a guess that the runner uses up more energy than the others!
Most children will have woken up very excited at the

prospect of their first gymkhana. For them it is a truly red-letter day and their accomplices do their best to help them enjoy it. Little legs flail against the ponies' sides as parents or elder brother or sister tug at the pony urging him to go faster and reach the finishing line first. There is nothing but smiles from most competitive children but occasionally they will dissolve into tears if they are too strung up, or if it is all a bit too much for them, or if they don't like losing. In the latter case it is a good thing to learn to be a good sport and that not everyone can win. If one of the former, the parent should think carefully before pushing the child into competition again too soon, in case it puts him right off and so he is denied the fun of riding that undoubtedly lies ahead.

Big things have small beginnings. How many young riders aspire to the dizzy heights of the world's best professional and Olympic show-jumpers? Those who feel impatient for fame and fortune would do well to remember that their super-stars began from scratch, and some of them from very modest backgrounds. To be a top show-jumper you don't have to have a rich father (although it may help as long as you have the ability and dedication to go with it). But those who come up the hard way often have most success in the end. That is because they have had to learn to get the best out of an ordinary pony and this in itself will teach them more about riding and jumping than any ready-made article. The child who gets eliminated but has the determination to keep trying may end up winning more prizes than the one who merely has to 'point and click', looking pretty on the perfect pony who takes him around faultlessly. Basic schooling should begin at home, probably over cavaletti. Here [*below*] a girl is taking a home-made practice jump perfectly with her pony, a broad smile showing her happiness, the pony's pricked ears indicating his enjoyment, too. Not everyone gets hold of manufactured show-jumps and anyway it can be great fun building your own. This is not a well-built obstacle. It has a flimsy top rail and not much in the way of wings, but it helps bring out the obedience and illustrates the willingness of a pony.

From here, if he wants to, a child progresses to a small show or local gymkhana. A course like this will not overface a pony at its first show, although it will take in many strange new sights and sounds and so could easily lose concentration, especially over a longer course than he has ever coped with before.

[*left*] Out in the wild two stallions fight each other and the winner takes control of the herd of mares. These young colts are domesticated but their play is reminiscent of the wild, where to play like this is all part of their preparation for the future when they would need to be able to fend for themselves. The buttercups in this field look pretty but they are a sign of inferior quality grass and not good for grazing.

The traditions of horsemanship are still strong in America, kept alive by the variety and popularity of the many events that can be enjoyed throughout the year. This foursome looks quite at home in their high Western saddles and cowboy headgear.
The degree of control that a cowboy has to have over his mount is quite consider-able as rider and pony have to form a bond of understanding in order to pursue and single out cattle for roping and branding.
Proof of this can be seen in the famous contemporary paintings of the West by Russell and Remington, two American artists who captured some of the colour and excitement of the cowboys' life.

More and more people are finding out what fun it is to go out hunting. During the school holidays there is always a large pony-mounted following. Britain and Ireland are the traditional bases of hunting but there are several packs in America and also in Australia where, in spite of the heat, they still wear the traditional clothes. A child needs to be reasonably proficient to go hunting because he will be riding across country where the going can be rough and the pace fast, therefore for the first few times he should be accompanied by an adult because there is so much to learn about the sport, and a pony allowed to do the wrong things will quickly get its young rider into trouble.

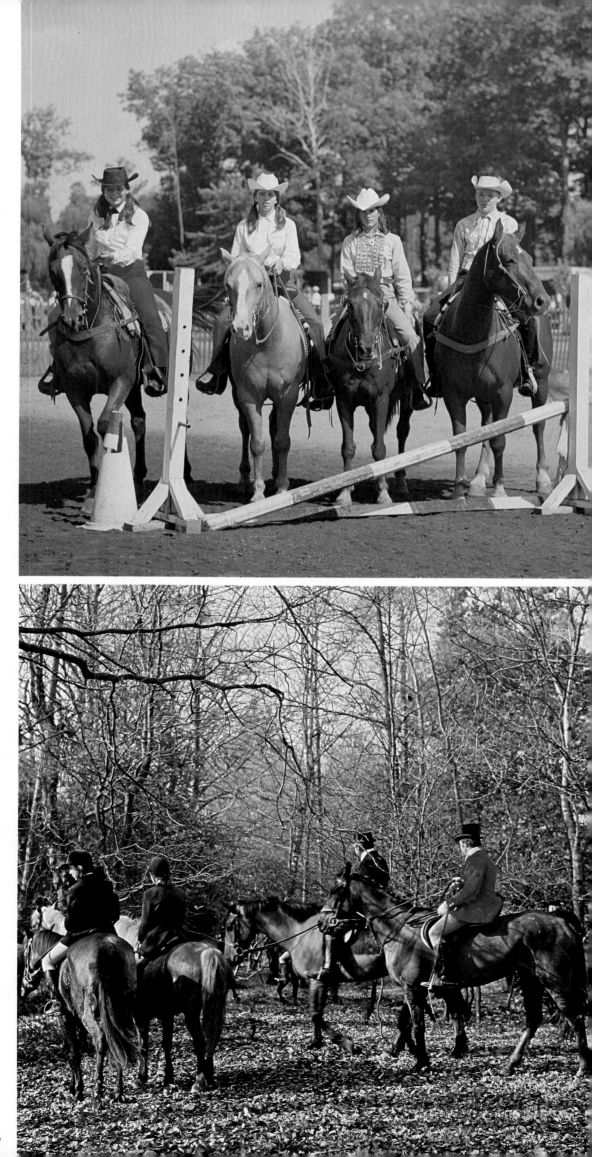

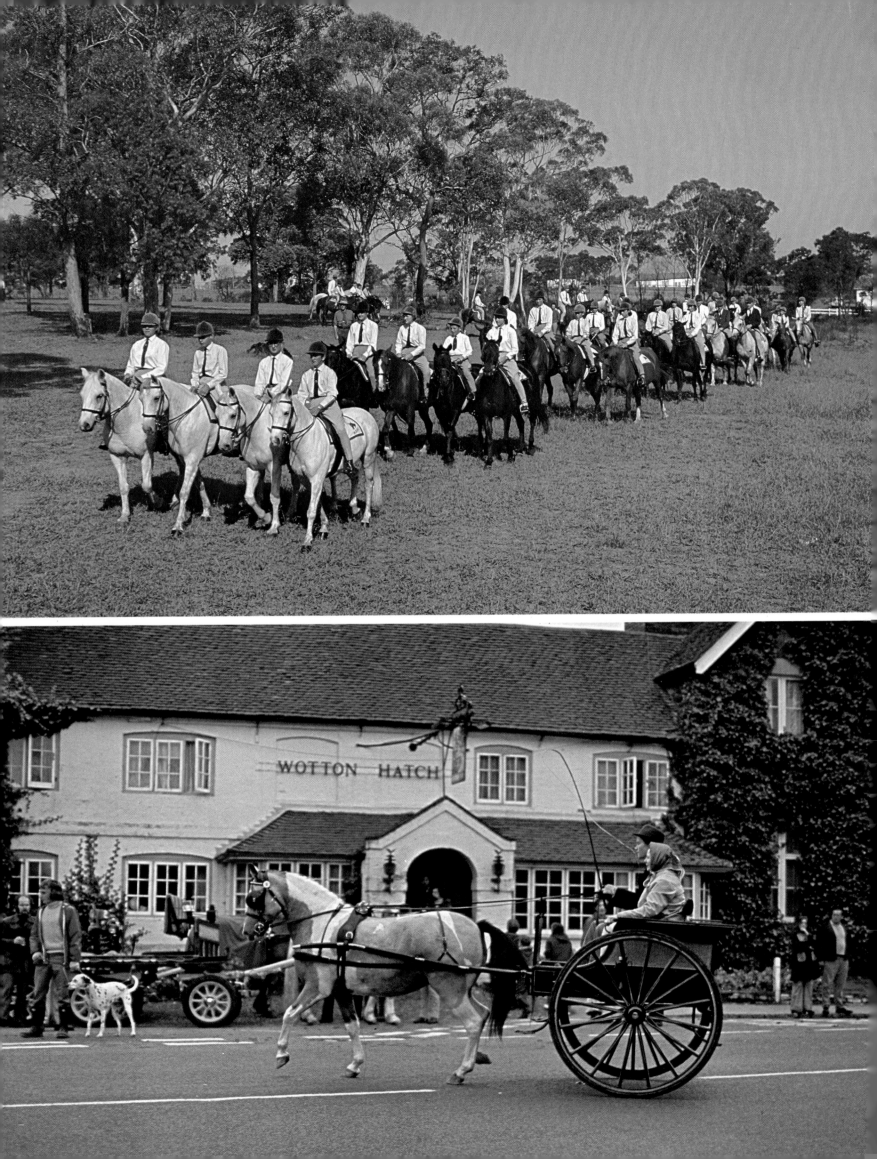

[*above left*] There are few Australian children who do not ride, many of them on cast-off stock horses or racehorses, and the country has a flourishing Pony Club with a membership of nearly 23,000. Here a troupe from New South Wales gives a polished display beneath a clear blue sky. Some branches of the Pony Club in Australia are more sophisticated than others, Melbourne, for instance, produces highly competitive children and ponies, who do well in three-day events.

For the children in the outback, Pony Club rallies may be more informal, but the essence is the same, to teach and foster good horsemanship and pony care. One thing the Australians can rely on is good weather for their events! Many of the town or city children hire ponies for the rallies and events. Those who do have their own, have considerable difficulty in finding grazing within reasonably easy reach of their homes, a problem which does not affect the country children who usually live on large rambling ranches.

[*left*] Here is something that looks lots of fun! This pony and trap are obviously well looked after, and what could be nicer than trotting down to the village inn on a Sunday afternoon. These traps were the product of great craftsmanship and care. In bygone days, of course, this was a normal mode of transport, but for today's car-age children it is a novelty; something that is seldom seen, even less experienced, by the majority of youngsters.

Having once tasted it, they may become keen to learn the art of driving as well as riding and that is not too difficult especially as you don't have to try to stay on! The reins are held in the left hand, and the right hand, which holds the whip, is only used on the reins for turning corners or, if in difficulty, to help pull up.

[*above*] The quadrille has become a popular riding pastime in recent years, and the finals of the British inter-riding clubs quadrille competition is now held at the Horse of the Year Show, Wembley. The teams choose a subject, dress according to it, and perform their movements to music suitable for the theme.

The quadrille is not in fact new. The first 'horse dances', as they were called, date from about 700–650 B.C. with two, four or eight riders taking part. There was then a gap of many centuries, but the quadrille was taken up again in the 16th century, the revival lasting until the 19th century. It was particularly associated with noblemen, and majestic courts throughout Europe could expect to witness displays of the highest standard and great elegance as the highly trained horses moved in time to the music. England did not see so much of them although they were encouraged during the reign of Queen Elizabeth I, Good Queen Bess. Now, during the reign of Queen Elizabeth II, it is far more the ordinary, everyday people with a love of horses who practise the art.

[*above*] Spring is here. The leaves unfurl to reveal a gentle green, the bluebells bloom and fill the woods with a sweet-scented, colourful carpet, the nesting birds sing merrily and the desire to ride is re-born in this young lad after the cold and wet of winter. This form of quiet hacking may be all that this boy asks for in the way of riding and to him and many like him it is sheer heaven. He may not like the idea of competing in public and may wish his mother would not push him to go to gymkhanas; or this

ride may be nothing more than a break between training his pony for the excitement of jumping and competing in gymkhana games. The pleasures of riding are felt in varying ways by different children, but whichever it is, one thing is for certain, contact with and care for a pony makes you feel good.

[*right*] America has seen a tremendous upsurgence in the popularity of Western Pleasure Riding which has spread to

England where it is now quite common to see riders wearing 'cowboy' clothes and riding on a Western saddle. One or two of them are even travelling around shows giving displays and demonstrations. Palominos, long known as the Golden Horses of the West, make the ideal partner for this sort of exhibition.

Many 'Western' riders use the *hackamore*, which is a bitless bridle and has two long metal cheeks curved to fit the nose and attached by leather. The horse is guided and controlled by pressure on the chin and nose.

The Western saddle is large and heavy, often with ornate trimmings and is rather like an armchair, designed for comfort on a long day's riding. But it is essential that it fits the horse or pony properly otherwise its weight will cause unpleasant sores. The reason the riders have their stirrups so long is again to be comfortable for all-day riding— try riding like a jockey all day and you will find it very hard to straighten your knees at the end!

[*left*] I make no hesitation or apology for including a picture of a fall in Ponies for Fun, for I have without doubt more often laughed about my countless falls than not, and I am sure the same applies for the thousands of children who ride for fun. Falls are an inevitable part of the game and nothing to fear. Indeed, many beginners will have heard the saying that 'you are not a rider until you have seven falls'. Usually children bounce straight back up again and so long as a child is not over-mounted he should not lose his nerve.

I remember being deposited on top of a fence like this in a hunter trial. As my pony peered down at me imperiously I am sure it laughed. I laughed too and thought the fence judge would find it amusing also but his face remained stony so I had no alternative but to quickly remount!

A pony is so sure-footed that he will seldom fall himself, but if it should happen on a road you must prevent him from struggling and causing himself more damage. To do this you should sit or kneel on his head and somebody else should provide something like sacking near his forefeet to give him a foothold. If you have ever wondered why those horses falling all over the place in cowboy films do not hurt themselves, it is because they are highly trained.

To begin with they are taught to lie down on a sand or sawdust bed, and this gradually progresses through the walk to the gallop. It does take an exceptionally courageous horse to do this and very high fees will be paid for those that do. The most important thing in a fall is to remain relaxed as this will result in less injury.

[*left*] Ponies are used for all sorts of things but here is an unusual sight! The scene is Germany and these pony mares, harnessed to a picturesque carriage, have got their foals with them at foot! It would be funny to see them trotting along the road with the faithful foals tagging along, unwilling to be separated from mums!

[*right*] Sheer heaven! Who can resist the appealing eyes and woolly teddy bear look that just begs you to cuddle him! But lavish devotion alone would not be enough for this Shetland pony for, like any domesticated animal, he needs regular food, water, care and attention. In return he will provide fun for all the family and I am sure that they will remember his antics affectionately for many years to come.

[*below*] The early American settlers depended on horses and ponies for pulling their wagons or 'Prairie Schooners', as the large covered wagons were called. Although the automobile has now largely taken over this role the old days are still fondly remembered. Fast highways, metalled road surfaces and mechanical 'horsepower' are no substitutes for sunshine, open countryside and a pony for a companion.

[*right*] Galloping across the sands in silver sunlight with all 12 legs off the ground one can almost feel the wind on the three riders' faces, the tingling sea air, and the glow of pure enjoyment. There is something wonderful about galloping beside the sea that fills one with joie de vivre. It is certainly felt by the pony, too, for at moments like this man and beast are as one, in complete communication. There is a feeling of freedom and elation.
There must be one note of warning, however, for beaches can have soft patches and if a horse or pony were to gallop into one at full speed it could suffer untold damage,

possibly injuring a tendon for life, or straining muscles necessitating weeks of rest. It might cause the pony to somersault. So it is best to know the beach, to walk along it one way first before cantering back the other. Racehorse trainers with access to the sea nearly always take advantage of it, and I know one trainer in the Midlands who every year travels his horses to the coast for an invigorating two-week break by the sea. A safe beach provides excellent gallops which need no maintenance, and a walk along the water's edge is a fine form of cooling off or a therapy for injuries. Red Rum, dual winner of the world's greatest steeplechase, the Grand National, had done all his preparatory training on the sands!

[*below right*] Salaah Day in Nigeria is a colourful event, for which horses and ponies are turned out in gay array. A Moslem festival, it celebrates the end of Ramadan, which is the ninth month of the Mohammedan year and is rigidly observed as a 30 days' fast during the hours of daylight.

Working Ponies

[left] As one business dies out so another is born. This has been the case with ponies as much as anything else. When the motor car came in, the future of the working pony seemed doomed, but as people found more time for leisure, so the pony was adapted by business-minded people to fulfil the new requirements. One of the most popular pastimes to spring up was pony trekking. Now holidays can be had in most beauty spots, on such vast tracts of wild land as can be found, for instance, in Scotland, Wales, Exmoor and Dartmoor, where the beauty can be seen and explored in the most relaxing way of all, on horseback. The word trek is Afrikaans for travel, and on ponyback you can go to places that are too rocky or steep for cars. The pastime is popular in several countries including Australia. Trekking caters for everyone from the most inexperienced riders upwards. Some centres are only for children, others only adults, but mostly the organizers mix ages and capabilities. Like riding schools, trekking centres should be approved, in this case by the Ponies of Britain Club, so if you want to feel sure that you are going to a reputable place where the ponies are properly cared for then it is best to go to one which you know to be approved.

Most treks will be for a day, returning to the centre at night in readiness for setting off in another direction the next day. A complete beginner can go, for the pace is usually a walk, and the pony, being carefully selected, will take good care of you, so there is nothing to worry about. Usually the local native ponies will be used for they will be the most suited to their own particular area. You will probably pause at a stream sometime in the day for the ponies to have a drink, and this will most likely be during the break for a picnic lunch, when the saddle is taken off, and the pony will not be ridden immediately after having a well deserved drink.

[below] Here is another way in which a pony is used for business, carrying those magnificent Turkish carpets for sale. Two small boys have charge of these mounts in the eastern Anatolia district of Turkey. Horses, ponies, and even camels have for centuries been used to carry these wares across eastern Europe and North Africa, trading them for other goods or money.

Many hundreds of ordinary ponies are kept not for fun but in a business, and one of the most common of these is a riding school. Although they will be in business for their owners they will nevertheless be providing pleasure for countless children learning to ride. Riding schools in Britain have to be licensed by the local authority following an inspection, which is carried out annually. This was brought about by the Riding School Act because, sadly, a number of riding school businesses were maltreating their ponies. Sometimes ponies that were only yearlings or two-year-olds were sent out for several rides in a day, and their ignorant customers did not realize that the ponies were being cruelly treated and made to work before their bones were grown and set. This is very largely not the case today, most proprietors realizing that to keep their clients coming, a well-run yard is essential. However any suspicion that all is not well should be reported to the local council.

The type of pony used in a riding school is almost certain to be a common one. For one reason, a business cannot afford to use the best animals on novices, and for another the common pony will be less likely to be temperamental or 'hot' than a near-thoroughbred. Luckily they are seldom exploited nowadays, in fact it may be more of a case that some staff are! For many establishments will employ pony-mad girls on the promise that they will prepare them for certain instructor's exams, calling them 'working pupils' or 'trainees', when in fact they are little more than cheap labour! It has been known for these promises of daily or weekly lessons not to be fulfilled. But again it is the minority which gets a bad name for the majority and a lot of well-run establishments give every chance to their pupils and produce young women highly capable of getting on in the world of horses.

Very often pupils are taught in arenas [*below*]. Here a group is going through the well-tried Heels down, Toes up, Elbows in, etc., formula. Once the basic rudiments of riding are mastered they will gain confidence to do more and more on horseback. One way of achieving a good, firm seat as well as good balance is to trot without stirrup irons and reins! [*below right*] It will make you feel painfully stiff the next day but the more you do it the more proficient and supple you will become! This pony is being lunged so that the young rider need not fear losing control. She is helping herself stay on by clutching on to the pommell of the saddle, and the lunge rein is attached to a cavesson over the bridle, so the bit is not pulled about in the pony's mouth.

Riding school ponies will work hard for their living but they are tough by nature and, so long as they are well cared

for in return, they will thrive on the treatment. They often have an advantage over privately-owned ponies whose owners may know little about their welfare for riding school ponies will, in licensed establishments, have a knowledgeable owner and plenty of company, which will at least be compensation for occasions when eager young riders may pull harshly on the bit or give conflicting 'aids'. Very often pupils will stay after a lesson to groom the ponies they rode or help clean tack, which is all valuable experience for when the day comes that they can own a pony of their own. Riding schools are found in most countries providing a wonderful opportunity for those who cannot have a pony of their own on which to learn to ride. Children on hirelings can often compete on equal terms with owner-ridden ponies at gymkhanas.

[*right*] Some of the world's most famous riders had their first ever contact with a pony on a pony ride at a fair or on a beach. When ponies are hired out for short trips, they are usually led if carrying very novice children. Really small children will be held on, too. The pony makes so many trips back and forth on its stretch throughout the day that soon it knows exactly where to turn without being told. Each ride will cost a few pence and by the end of the day the total will have swelled into several pounds.

Such rides are popular at coastal resorts or summer fêtes, or wherever a lot of children are likely to be clamouring for a ride. This little girl is obviously thrilled and awed at her ride. She is too small for her feet to reach the stirrups, so they have been put through the leathers.

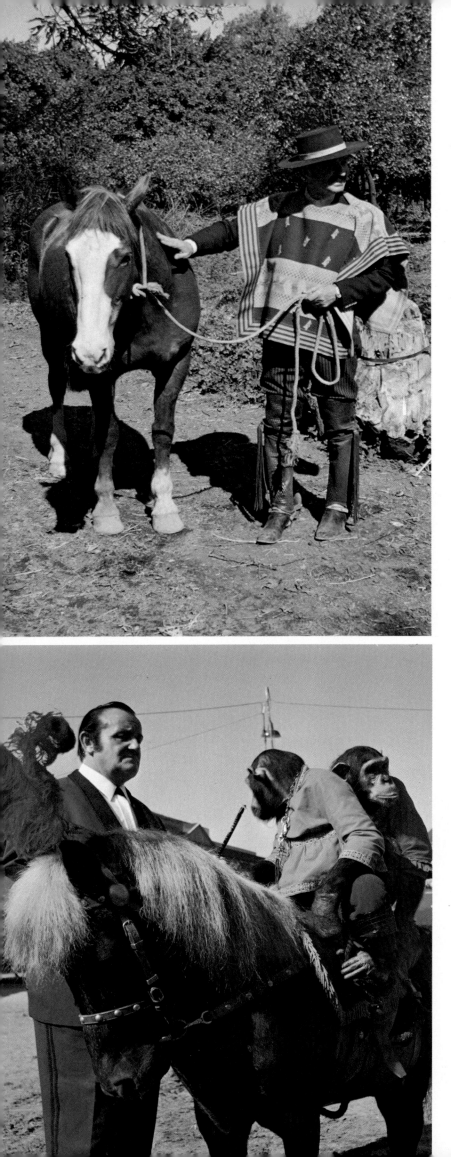

[*left*] Horses feature widely in the lives of people in South America too and here a pony helps this Chilean earn his living on the farm. If there is a rodeo in a nearby town, then horse and rider get dressed up and go off to take part in the festivities.

[*below left*] The delight of every circus is the pony. A big money-spinner, the first priority when choosing a suitable pony is his looks—he must be immediately appealing to the public who, in the main, will be non-horsey people and therefore primarily concerned with 'love at first sight'. For this reason the mischievous Shetland, with his impish eye, shaggy mane and tail, and cuddly woolly bear look, is always popular.
Circus ponies and horses will often go through 18 months to two years of training before ever appearing in public. They are seldom bought under four years old as their bones need to be set and strong before coping with the rigours of the circus act. They will get to know their trainer so well that a mutual bond of trust and respect springs up. The Liberty horses, which are chosen in matched colours, take nine to 12 months to train for their act which they carry out in the refinery of plumes and gay colours. They are usually stallions, since they arch their necks and have fine crests and carriage. Liberty ponies, possessing more independent characteristics than horses, often take longer to train. They must learn their name, and then they must learn to go to their trainer standing in the middle of the ring when he calls their name. High School, or Haute Ecole, horses take the longest to train for they perform the most intricate steps, but the Rosinbacks, the name given to the bareback act horses and ponies, are the quickest to train. Here the most important attributes are an easy temperament and a broad back, for they do not really have to learn any tricks, all they must learn to do is canter round the ring at the same steady pace no matter what sorts of antics are happening on their backs, or even, on occasions, on their necks and tails or under their tummies! Here a circus pony at an advanced stage of his training jumps a narrow, flimsy pole without hesitation at the command of his trainer who is several feet away. Even after he begins giving performances he will still have regular training sessions to keep him in trim.

[*above right*] Just as the Romans enjoyed chariot races, so Westerners still enjoy their chuck wagon races. Although fun, the element of danger is ever-present. A corner taken too fast can result in a 'spill'—in other words overturning your wagon. On the straight you can be racing wheel to wheel and only inches from disaster. These wagons are stripped down for speed; fully laden they must have stretched the 'ribbon handlers' skill to the limit.

[*right*] 'Roll up, roll up, who wants a ride!' Here there is all the fun of the fair and that includes rides in a gaily painted pony trap. The pony is in all his finery today but he probably earns his keep during the week by pulling a log cart or something similar for his master. Note the amount of 'feather' around his heels, a sure sign that he is a commoner. Thoroughbred ponies hardly have any hair on their heels. The fairground is the place to find lots of happy young faces and many of them will coax enough money out of their parents for a ride.

[*above right*] In any resort there will be tourist attractions, usually emphasizing an ancient local art or custom. Here we have a pony and painted cart with an exceptional amount of colourful trimmings, which will be used to take visitors around Palermo in Sicily. There is a lot of money to be made in tourism, and apart from pony owners like this vying for trade, the souvenir shops around the coast will be full of miniature models depicting these ponies and carts, besides a host of other attractive souvenirs.

Probably only a few miles inland, life will be sleepy and quiet under the blazing sun, much as it has always been, because few tourists seem to leave the sea and venture inland to see what the life is really like!

Meanwhile this pony will be kept busy throughout the height of the tourist season showing the established beauty spots to tourists. He will jog past the romantic beaches with their grottoes and caves, at the foot of great sweeps of olive groves and pine-wooded hills sloping away towards the majestic Mount Etna in the distance. Or he will wind his way through the narrow, flag-stoned streets of the town where bars, night spots and shops are clustered. Another route he may take his passengers on is to the various Greek and Roman ruins dotted about, and to several of the Norman churches and palaces which are to be found on Sicily, the largest of the Mediterranean islands.

[*below left*] Every year the coster ponies of London take part in the traditional Easter Monday parade in Regent's Park, and a fine sight they make, too. It is perhaps surprising that there are so many working ponies remaining in London, but they can be seen trotting along the streets in the early morning, going to and from the markets and then delivering wares such as flowers or groceries. Some work for rag and bone men and wait patiently outside houses while the master collects goods. The London Van Horse Parade Society was founded in 1904 when coster ponies and horses still made up most of the city's traffic, and its aims were to improve the treatment and general condition of van and light draught horses and ponies employed for business purposes, and to encourage drivers to take a humane and individual interest in the horses under their care. Almost like a union for the animals, one might say!

[*above*] Here is a smart turn-out. This pony is pulling a Victoria-type carriage. There is quite an art in driving well. Exponents of this art today emphasize the need for good hands and rounded wrists, but it can be quite easy to learn and if one is not born with naturally good hands it is possible to acquire them more easily when driving since there is not the added problem for a novice of trying to stay balanced in the saddle! Novice riders are often inclined to 'hang on by the reins', a habit which can only cause distress to the pony, unless it has become exceptionally 'hard-mouthed' through enduring too much of such treatment. That is why it is very helpful to learn to balance without the assistance of reins

Family Events

Never run before you can walk is as apt a motto for riding as anything else, for before you tackle those big fences at glamorous shows you must have learnt the rudiments both at home and at local shows. In this way you will gain confidence with your pony and, as your partnership improves, so you will make steady progress.

This [left] could be an open event at a local show and the combination is jumping in fine style. It is not fair to take your pony straight out of a field into a jumping competition. For one thing he would not be fit to do himself justice, and you could cause him unnecessary hardship by expecting him to do so and for another, as in all sports, time spent in training is never wasted. Groundwork and schooling over small cavaletti may seem boring but the rewards can be reaped in the show-jumping ring.

[right] The family pony should not be over-faced and here is a sensible way of beginning his competing life. His young rider has not pulled at his mouth and she is already looking towards the next jump. The pony's ears are pricked and he is obviously enjoying himself.

[below right] A year or so later they manage bigger fences. Here the pony does not need any gadgets to control him and he jumps freely. They say if you throw your heart over a fence a pony is sure to follow but I must confess there have been times when I have taken this too literally and found myself on the landing side with my mount's feet firmly rooted on the take-off side. On the other hand, a pony will often sense an unsure rider, so if the rider hesitates, the pony is likely to follow suit, whereas by 'throwing your heart over' your confidence is transmitted.

[*above*] Ponies can be enjoyed by the whole family, being passed down as they are out-grown. Here a group of friends are photographed on an assortment of mounts. Many family ponies will be of no specific breed other than 'common', yet they are honest, tough, willing and often less temperamental than their blue-blooded brothers, thus making ideal mounts for novices.

This group of young riders is enjoying the moors of Derbyshire with its wide open spaces.

[*left*] It is good fun to go riding for a day where you can keep away from too many roads and, when, by taking sandwiches and a headcollar, you can have a picnic lunch on your trek. If you take a map and pick your route, you will discover that so much more of the countryside and the wild life in it can be seen on a pony, because he can go where it is too steep or rough for a car or bike, and he can take you further than if you were on your own feet.

[*above right*] There is more than one way of utilizing the family pony, for instance in far-flung parts of Australia it can be used for transport to and from school, as is the case for this group near Towong in New South Wales. With satchels strapped to their backs the children carry all the school books they want. During school hours the ponies are tied in the shade.

New South Wales is the oldest and wealthiest of the Australian states, it is also the most densely populated, not that dense is an appropriate word in that vast country. Indeed, people in Perth, western Australia, can ask a friend in all seriousness if they know someone in Sydney, $2\frac{1}{2}$ thousand miles away, and the chances are they will! Outside the bustle of Sydney and its magnificent natural

harbour there are many isolated ranches like this one, where riding is a way of life for all members of the family.

[*below*] During school holidays it is lovely to fetch in your pony, brush off the mud, tack him up and take him out for a ride. These girls have an advantage because they live near the South Downs where they can ride along established bridle paths, along the South Downs Way, without ever doing more than crossing a made-up road. There are magnificent views of the English Channel to the south, and of the Sussex scenery stretching far away in the valley below. Certain preservationists have worked hard to keep these tracks open to the public and have a fine and worthwhile job which we can all benefit from.

[*above*] Is your bit of grass sweeter than mine? This pair of shaggy grey Shetland ponies graze peacefully among the oak leaves. Ponies like these are sometimes kept purely as pets, although, by and large, ponies really like to be ridden and kept in work as it gives them something interesting to do. It also prevents them from becoming too fat which in turn makes them unhealthy and bad on their feet. These look totally innocent but in fact Shetlands have quite a mischievous streak in them and have been known to disobey the commands of little riders! It is usual to find ponies grazing close together even when they have a large field to choose from. This is probably a heritage from the days when they had to keep

close together to warn each other when danger was near, but it is also, of course, because they like to have company. [*above*] Under or over? Ponies that have been handled since birth love contact with human beings. Even when they are turned out together for companionship they often come to the gate at the sound of a familiar voice in the hope of being taken out for a ride, or of receiving some titbit. Sugar is not really very good for them but apples and carrots are, and they love them just as much. Some ponies will play the devil when they are to be caught, running around just like naughty children not wanting to go to bed. However they can nearly always be tempted by some oats.

[*left*] Happiness is . . . a girl and a pony. Pert and impish, the pair can guarantee each other hours of fun and the whole family will be involved when they listen to stories of what the two have been doing together, or when Mum is required to prop up poles in the field or Dad is asked to drive them in a trailer to a gymkhana.

[*below left*] Who is working hardest? Part of this event in America involves these youngsters in leading their ponies round the circuit. Not everyone is meeting with equal success as brute force is no substitute for a well-trained pony.

One of the most popular events is always the mounted fancy dress parade. This is usually held after the lunch break when entrants have had time to get themselves ready. It makes an amusing start to the afternoon's proceedings and there are always some ingenious and colourful outfits on show. Many hours of work will have gone into some of the home-made costumes.
Here is a happy looking chap [*right*] and behind him can be seen a 'scarecrow'.

[*above*] Gumboots, old jeans and sweaters are the order of the day as the whole family arrives at the local show, for it may well be cold and muddy and a small gymkhana will not have concrete paths or permanent buildings to keep warm in. If a girl is taking her pony to the local show you can bet that younger brother will come along too to see the fun, Mum will be there to help hold the pony and to console the daughter when she does not do as well as she had hoped, and Dad will walk the dogs and meet a few cronies in the refreshment tent! Gymkhanas are informal, friendly affairs and an excellent way for children to get used to competition with its excitements and, very often, disappointments.

How well I remember my first gymkhanas. My first pony made a regular habit of bolting (when he wasn't bucking)

and a poor, frustrated mother had plenty of problems on her hands trying to cope with us both! The pony entered the jumping ring, jumped the first fence, and promptly bolted out of the exit, causing instant elimination. My second pony was just the opposite. No amount of kicking and vocal persuasion could get her to go faster than a sluggish trot. All this time my friends were winning more and more rosettes but I never lost faith in the ponies. I always loved them, and by the time my wonderful Welsh Cob came along to set me along a belated winning way I think I had learnt a lot more about riding difficult ponies than had my friends who until then had been doing all the winning on their perfect ponies!

[*left*] Picnic lunch, and the pony came too! Mother has brought all the paraphernalia with her in a basket and set out the tempting sandwiches, cold meat, pies, apples and bananas on the rug, with drinks of squash and flasks of tea at the ready. It is an ideal time to give the pony a break. It is a good idea to remove its saddle, but before putting it back on remember to brush out the dried sweat so that the pony is comfortable and ready to go on with the afternoon's events.

[*above*] The scene in the horse-box park is a hive of activity as the finishing touches are put to the pony before it is time to warm up, and then enter the ring. Mother lends a hand now, and will be giving moral support from the ringside as, a little later, she watches her daughter compete. Then it will be back to the box to hold him again while he is rubbed down, and has tail bandage and knee-pads put on before loading up to go home.

Competitive Ponies

There is a unique atmosphere to the Royal Dublin Horseshow. The mecca of horse-lovers, it is renowned for its hunter classes for which Ireland is still the premier breeding ground and the jumping, in the magnificent outdoor arena. People flock to Dublin to see the many different types of hunters judged, many of which will find new owners. A bloodstock sale is run in conjunction with the show when many racehorses change hands also.

Here [*above*] the Connemara ponies, Ireland's wonderful native breed (described earlier in the book), are lined up before the judge. Notice how many of them are grey in colour. They will be judged on their conformation, action and for trueness to type.

The jumping at Dublin is the high-spot for many up-and-coming competitors and here [*left*] a children's jumping competition is in progress. This young boy has got a bit 'left behind' as his pony leaped, his hat has flown off, and he is looking back to see if the pony has cleared the fence. But he has kept his pony's mouth free, and in turn the pony has tucked up his hocks so well that they are clearing the fence easily. This is often where a pony can be more clever than a horse, his agility making up for his lack of size.

Many famous jumpers have come out of Ireland, one of them being the diminutive Dundrum who, ridden by Tommy Wade, won many adult competitions against horses. Seamus Hayes and more recently Eddie Macken, two very popular Irishmen, have made the grade internationally, having begun on ponies in their home country. The most important jumping competition at the Dublin Show, which is held every August, is the nation's competition for the Aga Khan cup.

The main object of horse-shows is to maintain and improve the standard of horses and ponies and, indeed, of horsemanship. For this reason specific classes are held at shows everywhere and judging should conform to basic standards. There are some specialist shows, for example the Ponies of Britain Show which deals only with ponies of all the native and riding types, but an average show will have classes for novice ponies, show ponies of different sizes, mountain and moorland classes, hunters, Arabs, hacks, brood mares and young stock and, of course, jumping. The gymkhana events provide an outlet for non-show ponies to compete on equal terms and obedience and training are just as important there.

Children's riding ponies are judged on manners and conformation and those under 12.2 h.h., ridden by the youngest children, should be quiet and reliable. Very often a judge will have them brought out in front of the line-up one by one to give an individual show, to see that there is no 'nappiness' at leaving the others. The ideal show pony in this bracket will have a good length of stride. The older child, showing a 13.2 or 14.2 h.h. pony, will be expected to cope with a bit of spirit in a pony, moreover a higher degree of quality and performance is expected, although good manners are still important. Many of these ponies are miniature thoroughbreds, with dainty legs, high-class heads, extravagant action and superb proportion.

They are turned out immaculately, nurtured as much as any thoroughbred horse, and generally schooled to an exceptionally high standard.

After the initial walk, trot and canter, the judge will call them into line in order of her preliminary preference. Each pony will then be stripped of its saddle and brushed over by a groom, who comes in from outside the ring. The judge will then closely examine each one individually. Here [below] the rider raises her hand in front of her pony to make him look alert with ears pricked and standing squarely with all four legs set apart to give the best possible impression under the judge's scrutiny. The pony will then be walked up and trotted back in hand before the judge, before they are all resaddled and walked round for the judge to select her final choice.

In a pairs class, seen here [right] in Australia, one or two other factors are considered, for the ponies need to be well matched and to go well together as a pair, in addition to the other requisites.

[below right] The hackney pony is most distinctive for its high, exaggerated action and the way its head is held high and alert. Seen mostly in the show-rings of today, the hackney and hackney pony began life as tradesmen's animals because their exceptional trot was most useful on the streets when delivering goods around town or for the journey

from farm to market. A hackney pony does not exceed
14 hands (above that he is a horse). Originally known as the
Norfolk trotter or Roaster, most hackneys descend from
the Darley Arabian and were first bred in Norfolk in the
1720s. Records show that a hundred years later one hackney
trotted 24 miles in an hour, and another hackney, called
Nonpareil, was driven 100 miles in 9 hours, 56 minutes,
57 seconds!

[*overleaf*] Four keen, eager faces. There is seldom a pairs
show-jumping class, but for hunter-trials, where there is a
less confined space, they are quite popular. Ponies will
often jump better together, giving each other encouragement
and it is a good way of getting a pony going over a
cross-country course. Hunter-trials are usually judged on the
fastest clear round although some organizers, to discourage
children from unkindly riding their ponies flat out, set a
standard time. This can also have its drawbacks, though, for
it has been known for a child to jump the last fence with
too many seconds to spare, slow to a walk, and pass the
finishing line consulting a stop-watch! Ponies do not have to
be matching for a pairs class, as my sister and I once
found when, to our surprise, our Welsh pony teamed up with
father's prized hunter and, with the pony showing the way at
trappy places and the hunter giving a good lead at bigger
fences, we won the cup!

[*left*] It is never too young to start showing, as this lad illustrates as he manfully leads his pony up in hand. It looks as though he will grow into his jodhpurs as well as his pony in a year or so's time! The Welsh Mountain makes the ideal first show pony, before going on to a thoroughbred, while the Pony Club show is the perfect way to begin competitive life.

[*above*] The Royal Agricultural Society of New South Wales is responsible for staging Australia's biggest and most comprehensive show in Sydney every Easter. There is an enormous variety of competition covering all aspects of horses and agriculture and including rodeo and carnival to enliven proceedings still further for the thousands of people who flock there. It is an occasion when town meets country and the show provides both a shop window for its many visitors and something of a fashion parade, too, a bit like the races for Royal Ascot in England.

[*left*] Some ponies will jump much better across country over natural fences than the brightly coloured island fences in the artificial atmosphere of a show-jumping arena. A hunter trial is intended to test a pony's aptitude at tackling the different types of fences it might encounter in the hunting field and sometimes a hunting horn is blown as each competitor starts to give the true hunting pony a bit of extra encouragement. Very often a classy horse or pony will win by virtue of being able to gallop faster. But jumping does come into it, too! Sometimes riders will take their horses so fast vying against each other that they cause them to make mistakes, perhaps cutting a corner too fast causing the horse to run out.

Our family favourite, the old cob, came up trumps by taking advantage of this once. He jumped a clear round at his very best pace but, over the mile course, he was still a full minute slower than the fastest.

'Did you stop for a cup of tea on the way round?' the time-keeper joked when I asked him for my time. I would have loved to have seen his face when Toby was announced the winner, because all those faster horses had collected jumping faults during their race round!

[*right*] There is magic in the grace and elegance of riding side-saddle. It is an art that has been revived in recent years and is ventured into with enthusiasm by many girls. Women often ride side-saddle, beautifully turned out in immaculate habits, in the ladies' hack class at bigger shows and some girls ride side-saddle in pony show classes. Many people think that in days gone by all women and young ladies rode side-saddle but this was not so, for they are depicted riding astride as early as the 5th century B.C.! They were also shown sitting sideways on the off side.

There is a pottery illustration dated A.D. 620 of a woman playing polo astride, but during the reign of Richard II (1367–1400) Queen Anne, on state occasions, rode on a side-saddle, with her feet supported by a trestle plank. However, the present form of side-saddle was introduced in about 1500, probably by Catherine de Medici. This became the norm so that, right up until the 20th century, women riding astride were considered eccentric!

[*below*] Pony racing took place in England, chiefly in the West Country, under Pony Turf Club and Pony Racing Society rules, intermittently between 1928 and 1964. The height limit was 15 hands and once a pony had run under these rules it was debarred for ever from running under Jockey Club rules, the governing body of British racing. One of the best known meetings was held at Hawthorn Hill in Devon. There is still some pony racing in Wales and Scotland.

Informal pony racing sometimes takes place and in 1974 pony races were held at Ratcliffe on the Wreake, in Leicestershire, in aid of that village's church restoration fund. There were about nine runners in each of the races, which were designed for differing heights and riders' ages. A high standard was ensured since some of the competitors had travelled there from Wales.

Another attraction quite often staged as a fund-raiser is a midnight steeplechase. There are different ways of organizing such an event, but usually it will be open to ponies and staged over a small course with obstacles of something like straw bales which will probably be floodlit. There may be several races, or else heats followed by a final, and competitors often have to wear night-dresses, though these are usually donned over the top of riding wear! The original Midnight Steeplechase is said to have taken place in 1803 from the Cavalry Barracks at Ipswich to Nacton Church, some four and a half miles across country. These events are usually organized when a full moon is expected and they are always good fun, even if the standard of competition is sometimes not very high!

[*right*] Another competitive sport that is especially popular in America and Australia is trotting. Several attempts have been made to introduce it to England but it has received little support. Here a trotting race is in progress in Menorca, the little Balléaric island in the Mediterranean, where it is greatly enjoyed. There is considerable skill in trotting racing, for the lightweight cart that the horse or pony pulls can be easily overturned if, in the heat of the moment, a driver tries to cut a corner too tightly. Trotting presents a medium for gambling and at most meetings there is a big betting turnover. The races are often run as handicaps, but this does not mean carrying extra weight as it would in a flat race. Instead, horses considered less likely to win are given a certain number of yards start.

The sport has had a firm hold on many American devotees for years. It began during Colonial times and for a long time was considered the country cousin to thoroughbred flat racing, but now the standard-breds for trotting race in large urban areas inside lavish stadia, equipped with the most modern and luxurious facilities, with automatic starting gates and floodlights for night racing. It is still thought of as a sport for the people, as opposed to the Sport of Kings, flat racing, and it retains its rural atmosphere at the less formal meetings of the country areas.

[*below right*] A polo pony is always called a pony even though, since the abolition of the height limit, many of those taking part are really horses of as much as 16 hands. A polo pony is a type rather than a breed and Argentina is a great country for producing them. They need to be fast, agile, obedient with powerful quarters, good flexion and great courage, to cope with the rigours of the game. To suit all this it is usually the smaller animals which are best.

The game of polo is very ancient and is believed to have originated in Persia in the 5th century B.C. when the game resembled mounted tennis! It became popular in India in about 1850 where British servicemen stationed there quickly found a liking for it after three members of the 10th Hussars read about it, procured some sticks with crooked ends, got hold of a billiards ball, went out to their chargers, and proceeded to play! They introduced it to England in 1869, the first game being played in Hounslow, and in 1883 America took an active interest, since when it has become an international sport. The oldest polo club is the Cachar in India founded by some British tea planters in Assam.

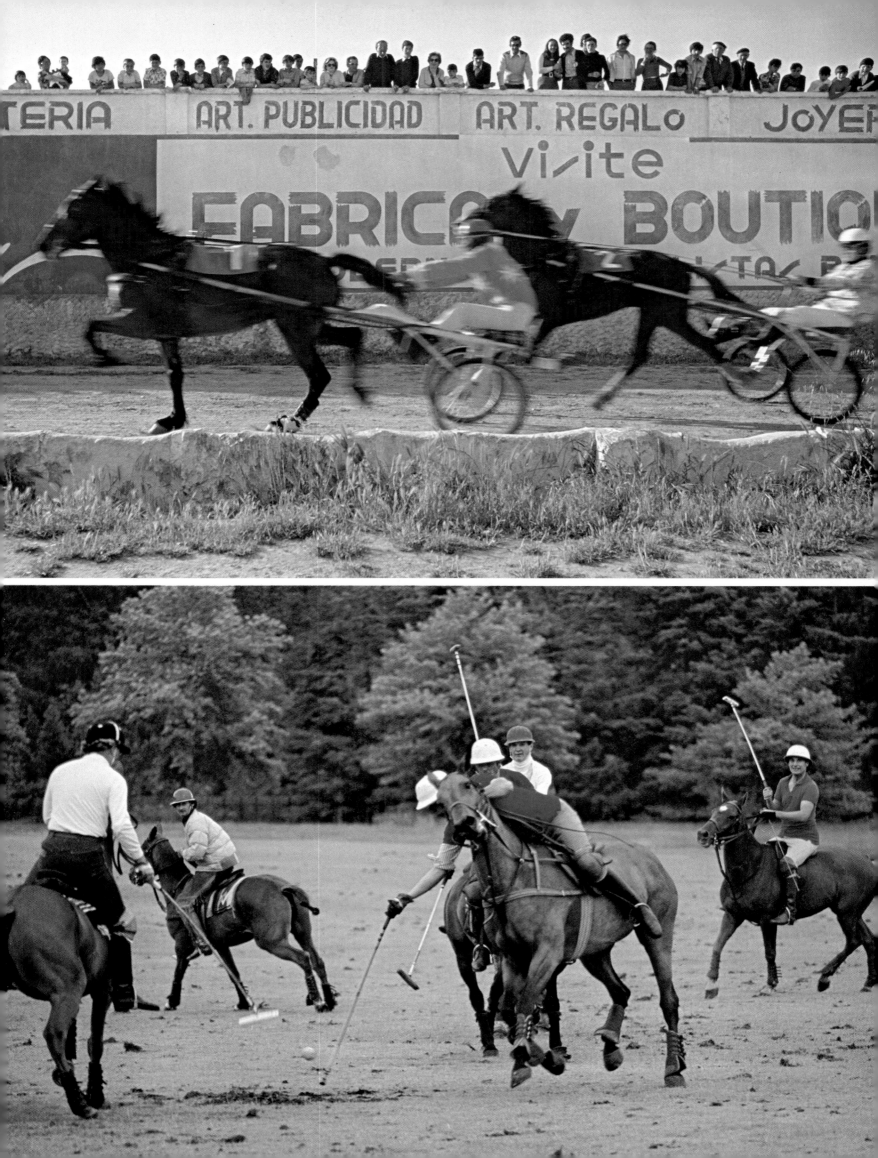

Care of Ponies

Here [left] is a well cared for group of ponies. There are many of them in one field but it is a large field and they are being given extra food by hand from a bucket. There are some fine big trees offering shade and shelter and the ponies look content. It is a strange thing that ponies turned out together in large numbers seldom get on badly with one another but if there are three in a field, two often gang up against the other one, especially if they are of different sexes. By contrast these Shetland ponies [below] have been left out under the blazing Argentinian sun with no shade and no food. But these hardy natives of the cold Shetlands look well able to thrive in these contrasting conditions. They are probably only put in this enclosure for a few hours each day for exercise and no doubt they are fed inside. It is incredible how these robust little creatures adapt. The Argentinians have, in fact, produced the world's smallest pony, the Felabella, by breeding down from the smallest Shetlands with the smallest Argentinian ponies, so the Shetland is now the second smallest pony in the world. The Felabella usually stands between 24 and 28 inches high (only 6–7 hands high!). The herd, which numbers about 400, was bred by Señor Felabella on a ranch outside Buenos Aires, where it runs on the pampas. They make wonderful pets, as they can be ridden by very small children and can draw miniature traps.

[*above*] 'No foot, no horse' is a well-known saying and one that is very true. It is most important to see that your pony's feet receive regular attention. This does not only mean putting on shoes, but, when the pony is out at grass, keeping the feet trimmed. There is nothing worse than to see a pony or donkey with its foot grown so long that the horn has curled up and the animal is hobbling around on the back of its heels. I have seen it and it is a distressing sight. When the pony is being ridden you will have it shod. If it is doing road work, the shoes will be replaced quite regularly because they will wear quickly, but if the pony is on grass and only ridden occasionally the feet will probably need attention before the shoes because the horn will have grown too long. The blacksmith will take off the shoes, trim the feet, and replace the shoes for you.
The method of 'hot' shoeing has long been favoured to nailing on cold shoes, because hot ones can more easily be knocked into the exact shape of the pony's feet and possibly tend to stay on longer. Here is a portable forge being used to deal with emergencies at a local show. A blacksmith is usually present at big shows, events and race-meetings. There is an almost acute shortage of blacksmiths in England.

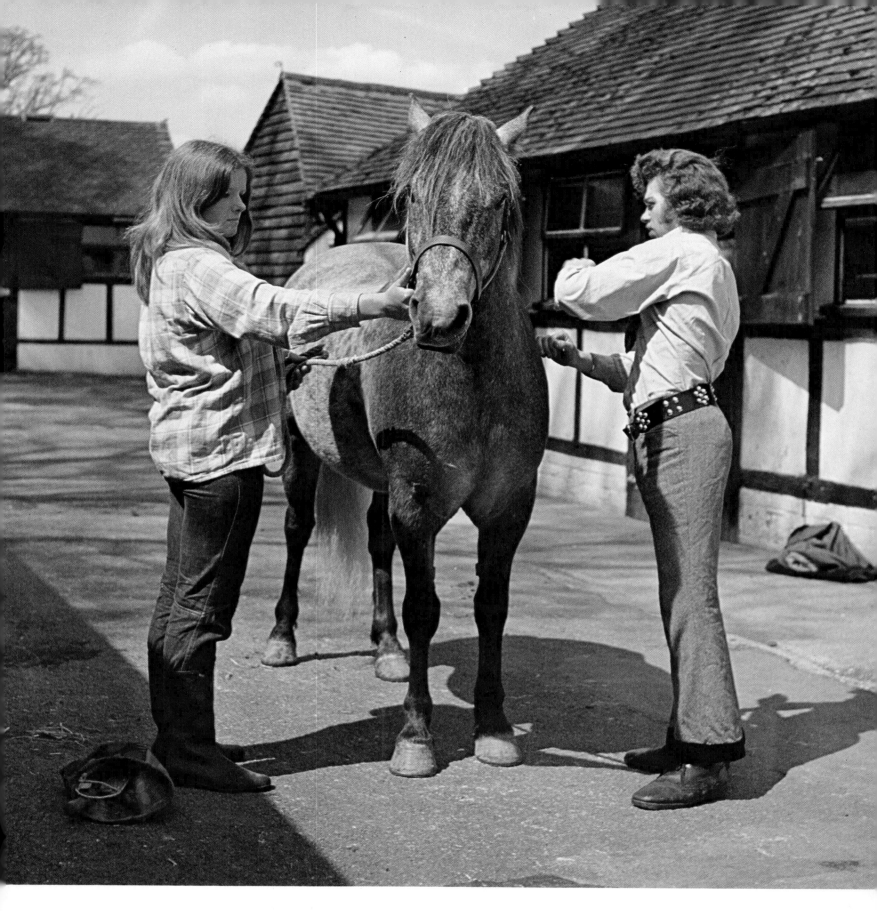

Gone are the days when one or two forges could be seen in every village. In some parts of the country you must travel many miles to have your pony shod. The reason is that when the motor car came in and before riding for pleasure became so popular, the number of blacksmiths dwindled along with so many of the work horses. Now there are the horses again and a crying need for more blacksmiths, but it takes a long time to train one and it is not always an attractive trade to the young men of today.

Sadly, some ponies fall into the wrong hands through no fault of their own and end up living skeletons. Countries like Britain, America and Australia have organizations which try to prevent or stamp out cruelty and promote kindness. Some places have sanctuaries, such as this one [*above*], where old or ill-treated horses and ponies can recuperate or spend their last days in peace. Once they are well cared for, they usually pick up enormously and the younger ones, instead of being prematurely retired, may be loaned to approved homes. Cases are brought in for a variety of reasons, often because of neglect, ignorance or cruelty. All are inexcusable for the result is the same: suffering for an innocent animal.

[*above*] One way of helping wild ponies in a difficult winter is to feed them hay, as the owner of these Dartmoor ponies has. Sometimes when a thick blanket of snow covers the moor in winter and sheep, in particular, are imperilled, a helicopter will drop supplies. Ideally, hay should not be fed to horses and ponies until they are one year old, and the best hay is that which can be made quickly and baled while it is still quite green. It would not be necessary to give the best hay to these ponies who have been used to the rough life. The highest tors on Dartmoor, which stretches for some 23 miles by 20, are Yes Tor and High Willhays, both of them over 2,000 feet high. The central part of the moor has been a royal forest since a date unknown, probably before the Conquest, and although there is not much actual forest left now—it is mainly bleak moorland—there are some areas of dwarf oaks on the lower slopes.

[*above right*] Most of the goodness in this grass has been scorched out by the blazing Australian sun, but the horses and ponies on this stud in Victoria, one of Australia's wealthiest states, have been well cared for. The eucalyptus trees are typical of the scenery. Originally, it was the discovery of gold which brought riches to Victoria and one of the little villages to spring up as a result was Melbourne, destined to become the capital. In the northern and central states of Australia, where droughts are common, farmers use horses and ponies to round up their cattle which have been roaming at will across territories the size of some European states! The pony can go where no car can reach, helping the farmer to look for lost sheep and inspect his fences.

[*right*] Playful nip! Here is a pony in good condition and you can see his tack has been carefully looked after, too. Ponies will sometimes nip when they are being girthed up if it is being done too sharply and pinches them. It should be a gentle process and the girth should be eased up gradually to tighter holes rather than jerked up. Then two fingers should be run down between the girth and skin to smooth out any wrinkles to make him comfortable. Some ponies 'blow' themselves out when they are being girthed, then, when you try to get on, the saddle slips round because they have let out their breath again! Sometimes when a pony has been hurt by pinching girths he will get into the habit of nipping from which it is hard to break him.

[*left and below*] Part of the fun of owning a pony, or of caring for one that you may ride at a riding school or friend's place, is in grooming it and enjoying the satisfaction of bringing out a shining coat.

The mud and dirt is best got out of a thick coat by a dandy brush, although this coarse brush is sometimes too ticklish for a thin-skinned thoroughbred or clipped-out pony. Having given your pony a good brush with that you are ready for the body-brush, when again you use strong, circular strokes all over the body, cleaning the brush as you go with a curry comb (which should not be used on the pony at all). Finally, a rub with a stable rubber helps bring out a good shine. When used on racehorses this cloth is thumped down with pretty good bangs helping to massage and tone the skin as well as clean it. Then you must pay good attention to the feet, picking up each one and carefully cleaning it out with a hoof pick, then brushing the outside of the hoof with oil, which helps to prevent them from cracking and also makes them look nice. Carefully wipe out the eyes and nostrils with a damp sponge, brush the mane and tail with the dandy brush and if you use a comb do not pull harshly with it. The result will be a beautifully turned out pony to be proud of and admired.

[*above*] Ensuring that a pony's tack is kept clean plays almost as important a part in pony care as does looking after the pony itself. Without daily cleaning the leather will become hard and cracked, not only shortening its life, but causing saddle sores on the pony where the stiff leather has chafed him. Leather needs to be kept soft and supple. This means using one of the makes of leather soaps and rubbing it well in, having first wiped off any mud or dirt with a damp cloth. It not only is better but it looks better, too. Stirrup irons and bits should be cleaned with a metal polish, again having first wiped off any mud.

The tiny and incredibly beautiful island of Lundy lies
12 miles off the north coast of Devon at the mouth of the
Bristol Channel. Besides its profusion of wild flowers which
makes the island, only three miles long and half a mile wide,
shimmer like a jewel, the wild birds all over it, the seals along
the coast and the goats and sheep grazing between the
outcrops of granite rock, there is also a small herd of ponies.
They are not indigenous but spring from a foundation of 34
New Forest mares let loose there in 1928. Even then the
herd did not establish itself quickly, for those mares turned
out not to be in foal and then an imported thoroughbred
stallion was found to be infertile. The first successful
stallion was Welsh and since then a Connemara stallion and a
half-bred hunter have added to the mixture. The offspring
have proved to be useful, hardy all-round types with good
temperaments, jumping ability, and exceptionally

strong feet caused by constantly walking over the granite rocks. The small island could not cope with too many ponies and so to prevent overcrowding and in-breeding the poorer specimens and the young colts are taken off the island each autumn, sometimes swimming on a tow rope behind the boat, as in the picture here. This practice could not be carried out during the last war, causing problems such as overcrowding, fighting among the stallions and a shortage of food, but now there is a resident herd of about 20, which is considered to be the optimum number.

There are prehistoric remains on the island, the foundations of an ancient chapel of St. Helen, and a Marisco castle which is in ruins except for its keep. French privateers used the island as a hiding place in the 17th century and, luckily for its future, when it came up for sale in 1969 it was acquired for the National Trust and so saved for posterity.

[*above*] This is the most usual way to mount. You should take hold of the reins with your left hand to prevent the pony from walking away, face the pony's rump, put your left foot in the stirrup, take hold of the cantle of the saddle with your right hand, and swing yourself aboard. Other ways of mounting are to use a mounting block; to be given a leg-up which is the normal practice with jockeys before a race; or to vault up, which is the way most racing lads mount on their way out to exercise as it means a keyed-up racehorse does not have to wait standing still. It is very useful for a child to learn to vault on, since apart from keeping him agile it will give him a great advantage in gymkhana events, where speed is of the essence. But for normal everyday mounting it is important to train your pony to stand still for you, as it is considered ill-mannered if he tries to walk off in the middle of the process. It can make all the difference to the result of a show pony class, too, for if the judge has difficulty in deciding between the first two, he may ask

the child to dismount and mount, and the one who does it best with the best behaved pony may be the winner.

[*above*] These happy girls are fitting a general-purpose saddle on their pony, and this would be the most usual sort for everyday riding and competing. There is, however, a wide variety of saddles ranging from the ½lb paperweight racing saddle for use by weight-conscious jockeys, to the huge, embossed Western saddle with its deep seat, high cantle and pommel, and big stirrups. In between, there is the straight-cut show saddle to show off a pony's shoulders, the forward cut show-jumping saddle with knee rolls, the felt saddle for a very young child, and even the basket saddle for babies which, as the name implies, is a wicker-basket seat to hold the baby safely, secure of course, with the usual girths. It is thought that the saddle was first put into use in the fourth century by the Byzantians, although they may have taken the idea from the hordes of Barbarians who, mounted on their horses, threatened the Roman Empire.

Horse and pony fairs up and down the country are quite a usual way of buying and selling the more common types of pony. Usually they are sold in an auction ring but here [*above*] they line a street centre. Sales in certain areas deal with particular breeds, for instance the Bampton Fair in Devon deals with the sale of Exmoors, the Beaulieu sales with the New Forest ponies, the Lerwick and Baltasound sales on the Shetland Isles with their native ponies, while the Stow Fair in Gloucestershire caters for a mixed bag. Stow-on-the-Wold fair, set in the heart of the lovely Cotswolds with its picturesque stone walls and buildings and fine hunting country, is one of the oldest. It was granted a charter in 1476 by Edward IV allowing the town to hold two fairs annually, each to last four days, 'with all rights, profits and advantages provided they be not to the hurt of neighbouring fairs'.

[*right*] At Bampton crowds turn out to enjoy looking at the mealy-muzzled Exmoors and watching the sales as much as taking part in them. The ponies are herded into pens and tickets showing their sale number are tied to their manes.

There is no confusion over the identity of the owner of such ponies, in spite of the fact that they have all roamed the moors freely together, because they have been branded as youngsters, before they are weaned, and so they are certain to be with their mothers who had themselves been branded with the owners' mark when they were at foot. Bampton is a fair that is even more ancient than Stow. It is a one-day fair held annually in October and it dates from 1258. Coloured ponies, that is skewbald or piebald, may be expected to make a little more money than some of their mates simply because of their eye-catching colouring, which makes them very popular with children. The scene is a similar one at the Beaulieu Road Sales, near Lyndhurst, in the heart of the New Forest, where sales of the native ponies are conducted periodically under the auspices of the New Forest Pony and Cattle Breeding Society. Some 600 or more Shetland foals are sold at the annual October two-day sales at Lerwick and Baltasound and the auctioneers, Shetland Marts, arrange for the foals to be shipped to Aberdeen after the sales, although from then on it is the new owners who take charge.

Breeding

[*left and right*] There are specialist studs
throughout the world and the
palomino is a popular pony for
breeding in America and England.
The palomino is not, in fact, a breed but
simply a colour, golden with flaxen
mane and tail. This makes breeding it a
more uncertain business than other
ponies; if, for instance, you put a
thoroughbred with a thoroughbred you
are certain of a thoroughbred foal
but two palominos may produce you a
cream or a chestnut foal. The most usual
ways of producing palominos are to use
both parents of that colour, or to mix
palomino, chestnut, cream or albino.
The only certain way of producing a
palomino foal is to use palomino and
albino parents, but this often results in a
rather flat, dull colour in the foals,
instead of the traditional colour
'the glint of newly-minted gold'.
Known as the Golden Horse of the West,
the palomino is really attractive and
eye-catching. Its origin is remote but
may well have been Arab and could
date back to the Homeric age. In
ancient chronicles it is mentioned as
being popular with the Kings of Yemen,
while in Spain, Queen Isabella, who
was to sponsor Christopher Columbus,
encouraged their breeding. The name
probably derives from one Juan de
Palomino. Besides being an excellent
saddle horse, the palomino makes an
impressive parade or spectacle horse and
is becoming very popular for Western
pleasure riding.

[*below right*] In the wilds of the New
Forest a native stallion leaps a gulley.
His qualities of toughness and
endurance will be passed on to the foals
his mares breed. It is a question of the
survival of the fittest in these conditions
and as he has withstood bitter winters
and harsh living in his natural
environment, so will the best of his
offspring. Thus the strain maintains and
improves its standards. There is not
the sheltered life of work in a stud for
these stallions and mares, but
nevertheless they thrive and casualties
are fairly few, because nature has her
way of looking after them.

[*right*] A shining example of healthy breeding: this gleaming Arab mare and her foal graze contentedly. Note that the foal has been introduced to a headcollar or foal slip already. This is an important part in his early education since, by becoming used to it almost from the start, some struggles later on are prevented. In the first few days of his life a foal should be well handled. It is important that this is done correctly, placing one arm behind his rump and the other in front of his chest (*not* his neck which could cut off his breath) to handle him out to his paddock behind his mother. The headcollar can be put on after a few days, but don't lead him by it for a few more days yet. Instead get him used to being handled everywhere else, because if you go to pull at his head too soon it will cause him to draw back and that could be a difficult habit to correct in later life.

The Arab is the purest and finest horse in the world. It founded the thoroughbred and it has a constitution of iron and exceptional soundness. There are many fine Arab studs throughout the world, the purity of the breed having been preserved by the zealous way in which the horses were guarded by the Middle Eastern countries, all the time from 5,000 B.C.! Besides being the oldest, most sound, and purest of all horses, the Arab is undoubtedly the most beautiful, with its refined head, broad forehead, large wide eyes, pricked ears, flared nostrils, distinguishing dished face, beautifully proportioned body and brilliant, free, swinging action which gives a wonderful ride. While the thoroughbred excels over the Arab for speed, the latter has supreme staying power.

All British racehorses descend from just three Arabs, the Byerley Turk (1689), the Darley Arabian (1705), and the Godolphin Arabian (1720), while all grey thoroughbreds descend from one horse, the Alcock Arabian of some 250 years ago (nothing to do with the author!).

An Arab can be any height but is usually between 14 and 16 h.h. Curiously, in the same way as a Polo pony is called a pony no matter how big he is, so an Arab is called a horse no matter how small he may be. It is difficult to give an exact height between horse and pony, but 14.2 h.h. is generally accepted as the top height for a pony (except 14 h.h. for a hackney pony).

[*below*] One of the important things to remember when you breed a foal is to ensure you have adequate fencing. This might look a sweet picture of a foal but just imagine if something startled him and he jerked his eye into that piece of protruding wire; or if in his gambolling he half fell through the gap in the fence and became straddled in it. The damage could be permanent or even fatal. An alarming number of horses or ponies acquire scars as foals which will always be a detriment to their appearance and which, with just a little care, could have been avoided. Even where there is good and safe fencing for your mare and foal you should still inspect it regularly in case of any damage needing prompt repair.

Gypsies have always been known as horse dealers. They also tell fortunes, make and sell baskets and clothes' pegs, and sell flowers, especially the women, whose style of dress includes kerchiefs over their heads, gold coin necklaces round their necks and gay dresses. Gypsies all descend from India and have a swarthy, dark appearance, although now they are scattered over many parts of Eastern and Western Europe. Many went to America in colonial times and even more at the end of the 19th century. They preserve their stories, songs and poems in their own Romany tongue. Their love of colour is illustrated by their brightly-painted caravans. Many attempts have been made to settle and educate the nomadic gypsies but largely without success. They have learnt their crafts and traded off them; they are knowledgeable about herbs—and they know a lot about horses. A stallion in Britain must have a licence but breeding goes on among gypsy ponies if they leave a colt ungelded. The gypsies find it useful to supplement their earnings by allowing the full-grown pony to undertake stud duties on the side, in addition to using them for pulling the caravans.

No mare and foal should be far away from water, and there is plenty of clean, fresh water here in the New Forest. If you have a pony and foal kept in a field at home make sure that you check the water twice a day to keep it filled up, even if you have an automatic system you must still look at it daily in case it goes wrong. When you embark upon breeding from a pony, perhaps from the old favourite you grew up on and enjoyed gymkhanas with, or a pure-bred native or show pony, remember they will need a regular change of grass. Two fields will not be enough because when you come to wean the foal you will want at least a whole field separating the two. Even if you have two fields which are not adjacent you still need a third one so there is always a fresh supply of grass. Constant grazing soon makes a field go sour or 'horse sick' and it will harbour the red worm, a virulent worm which will make a pony go thin and lack-lustre and must be treated. When you bring your pony back from visiting the stallion and have 11 months to wait, it is wise to turn her out with a quiet, sensible companion so that the mare will not gallop about too much.

[right] Youngsters at play, an important part of growing up. They will often rear up and paw at the ground or at each other in their games, this precedes a gallop around bucking and kicking and thoroughly enjoying the joie de vivre. There is no harm in their antics and they will not hurt each other. They quickly become weary of their games so they do not over-exert themselves, and end with a nice roll in a patch of mud, or with a quiet spell grazing close to their mothers or nuzzling up to each other for a scratch. This pair have plenty of room to romp around in. The grass is not wet, the sun is shining and life is one long, round of fun.

[*below*] In spite of the rigours of living in the middle of the Black Mountains of Breconshire this mare looks a picture of health, so too does her foal as he peeps round his mother's legs to take an inquisitive peep at the world. There is no special diet for him nor forced weaning; the mare eats as much good grass as she can find so that she can produce plenty of milk for him. Soon he will nibble a few blades of grass and weaning will become a natural, gradual process over several months.

[*below right*] The care and forethought which will have gone into the breeding of a top class show pony is infinite. Although such a pony can be bred by fluke and with little attention by human beings, it is a rare occurrence. To begin with, the choice of a stallion must be carefully made and it would be almost futile to use an inferior mare. One's good points should be used to rectify the other's bad points, and here the stallion exerts most influence. For instance, if the mare should have a poor head and the stallion a fine one, the foal will in all probability have a fine one. If both mare and stallion have a fine head, then the foal's head should certainly be excellent. But it would not be fair to expect a stallion, however fine, to produce something good if just about everything is wrong with the mare's conformation, soundness and overall good appearance.

Having chosen the mate, the mare owner should not then 'leave it all to nature'. That is all very well in the wilds, but these ponies have been nurtured since babyhood so it is more important than ever to carry on now, especially by supplementing the grass with feeds in the winter such as oats, and when she comes near to foaling add bran mash and some linseed, too. Some years later the rewards of this care may be reaped in the show ring, quite apart from the satisfaction of knowing at the outset that the best is being done to provide for the future.

Some mares will surprise you and others will keep you waiting for days or even weeks when you think things look imminent. We once miscalculated a valuable thoroughbred mare's time and, before she was showing any of the usual signs, she produced a strapping great colt without any complications, in the paddock one night—but we were lucky. Another owner was not on the spot; he made a late night check and visited his foaling box a mile away first thing in the morning. He found the foal born dead, yet if expert help had been on hand it would undoubtedly have lived.

For this reason it is often advisable to send a mare to stud where an experienced stud groom is on hand and will stay up all night if foaling seems imminent.

Champions and Celebrities

The only show class in which ponies are expected to jump (as opposed to jumping classes) is the working hunter pony. He is not only meant to have the good looks and straight action of the show pony but he is also supposed to be a good performer in the hunting field. To test this ability, he is required to jump a small course of rustic fences, as closely resembling those encountered out hunting as possible and nothing like the bright colours of show jumps. He may have a little more bone and stronger shoulder and quarters than the show pony, but he still must not be heavy. Here [*above*] is a perfect example of the working pony and in a very attractive setting too.

[*right*] A champion at the Royal Easter Show, Sydney, this pony, bedecked in garlands of glory, parades in front of the crowded stands. It is the most important show in Australia and just to win one class there is a high accolade, let alone several! It is an occasion to rival all other social events in the Australian calendar, with visitors travelling from far and wide to reach it and see the cream of the country's horses.

[*left*] Prince Charles, the Prince of Wales, followed his father's love of playing polo and has become an adept and proven player, although his royal commitments and career often prevent him from taking an active role in as many fixtures as he would like.

Prince Philip, the Duke of Edinburgh, did much to capture the general public's imagination in the game, and he ranked third in the British Isles in the 1950s. An injury forced him to retire in 1971 but luckily Prince Charles had become a keen player by then, so the public could still follow the royal progress in the game. More about polo as an ancient sport has been said on page 62.

H.R.H. Princess Anne has always loved ponies and far from outgrowing the 'pony mad' stage, riding became her greatest dedication in her limited leisure time, culminating in the stupendous achievement of taking the individual World Three Day Event Championship title.

Like many ordinary little girls, Princess Anne started her competition life in local gymkhanas. It was when she went to boarding school in Benenden, in the Weald of Kent, that her riding improved by leaps and bounds. This was helped tremendously by the fact that Moat Farm Stables were right next door, where, under the expert guidance and tuition of Mrs Cherrie Hatton-Hall, an excellent foundation was laid, on which her present trainer, Mrs Alison Oliver, was able to build after Princess Anne left school.

This picture [*below left*] illustrates what a good 'firm seat' Princess Anne developed from an early age. She is in perfect unison with this skewbald pony and has him well collected and balanced as she canters round a bend in the jumping arena. When Princess Anne first started competing in one-day and three-day events she was always thronged by admirers and here [*above right*] she can be seen patiently showing her pony to two young girls. Proud mother and happy daughter [*below right*]. A moment in a million as H.M. the Queen presents the trophy to the world three-day event champion, her daughter. This historic event took place in 1971 at Burghley and the horse which carried her to victory was a home-bred chestnut called Doublet, by Doubtless out of a polo pony mare. One criticism that could never be levelled at Princess Anne was that she gained her success 'because she was a rich man's daughter'. Just the opposite prevailed, she really earned it because she worked exceedingly hard at it in the moments she could snatch away from official business and then competed on level terms with competitors, some of whom had been bought expensive ready-made mounts and who could then spend all their time with them. It must have made Princess Anne's achievements all the more satisfying because they were gained on a home-bred horse that she had trained herself, as has been the case with most of her horses.

One such was a grey by Colonist called Columbus. A strapping big horse, he was really too strong for the Princess, but then the man in her life came along, and Capt. Mark Phillips struck up a fine partnership with him. In the spring following the young couple's marriage in Westminster in November 1973, Capt. Phillips and Columbus won Badminton. Then in the autumn of that year he was on the point of achieving a unique family double when fate struck a cruel blow. In the World Three Day Event Championships, back again at Burghley, he was in the lead on Columbus after the dressage and crucial cross-country. He had only to jump a good round show-jumping but unfortunately Columbus became a bit lame and had to be withdrawn, depriving Capt. Phillips, a former Pony Club member and member of the British Olympic squad, of an outstanding opportunity.

Princess Anne has an all-round interest in horsemanship, and in eventing her horses nearly always perform a polished dressage test. She makes sure she is fully fit for the cross-country herself, too. In fact, some years ago, she worked extremely hard to make herself fit for and ride in an event only a few weeks after an operation. It is this sort of dedication from which true champions are made. Her official functions have enabled her to see horses and ponies in all corners of the globe. She has ridden the famous Haute Ecole Lippizana horses of the Spanish Riding School in Vienna, she has ridden to the Chinese border while visiting Hong Kong, and she is a conscientious president of the Riding for the Disabled Fund. Here [centre left] the smiling Princess is seen competently driving a pair of Haflinger ponies, her young brother, Prince Andrew, at her side.

[*left and right*] The rise to fame of Debbie Johnsey was little short of meteoric. By the time she was 11 years old, when most children of that age are content with competing in local shows, Debbie and her fabulous pony stallion Champ VI had done so well that they were selected for the British Junior Show Jumping team, along with three teenagers. Then it was found that under European rules there was a minimum age as well as a maximum one, so Debbie had to wait until she was 14 years old before eventually she could be chosen to represent her country in international competition, but she quickly made up for lost time and still had the wonderful services of Champ VI. She and her pony were trained by her father in their Chepstow home and they added the British Junior open championship at Hickstead to their laurels. When Debbie graduated to a horse it was the highly priced but difficult ride called Speculator. With him she entered adult competition of the highest class and in 1973 she only just failed to take the Queen Elizabeth Cup, the top women's competition at the Royal International Horse Show, finishing fourth.

Debbie has a younger sister called Clair, to whom the fabulous pony Champ VI was passed on. She has already sealed an indelible mark on the show-jumping world, showing the same courage, dedication and determination that take a young rider to the top as her sister did.

[*below left*] Young champion at home. When she was 11 years old, Elizabeth Boone won 200 prizes in two seasons of horse shows with her Welsh 12.2 h.h. pony Coed Coch Buddai. He helped her develop her passion for eventing, winning a Pony Club event four years running. Even more famous was her 14.2 h.h. Treeyews St. Columba who won the area Pony Club trials individual title no less than six years running, and was runner-up for the junior show-jumper of the year at Wembley. Then she graduated to a horse and, with Off Centre, helped Britain to win the European Junior three day event championships. Elizabeth has other nice young horses which she is bringing on from her Norfolk home.

[*right*] Chepstow, Monmouthshire, has also produced the world famous show-jumper David Broome. Here his younger brother, Fred, is seen following in his footsteps riding Wenlock Wolf at Hickstead, the All England jumping course in Sussex. The sons of a farmer, the Broome brothers are country people. They have received much encouragement from their father, himself an accomplished horseman, in their show-jumping.

David Broome has competed in four Olympic Games, twice winning an individual bronze medal on Sunsalve and Mister Softee, and has been European champion three times and world champion. A true amateur within the meaning of the word, David now runs the family hay and straw business. Younger brother, Fred, may well become as famous a show-jumper, judging by the way he has started.

Two worthy champions. This very fine
Exmoor specimen [*right*] clearly shows
the mealy muzzle of the breed, with
mealy markings on the eyelids above and
below the wide-set, kind, liquid brown
eyes (known in the West Country as
'toad eyes') and the thick mane.
[*below right*] This Highland pony has
taken nearly every championship open
to him at this show. A champion is
not the winner of every class in a show,
but normally of a defined group, such as
Mountain and Moorland breeds, or
in-hand hunter youngstock, and the
first and second prizewinners of the
classes in the group qualify for their
respective championships. If it is a big
show there may be a Champion of the
Show, for which the selected champions
of each group, would qualify. It can
be a very difficult task to judge the
overall champion because of the widely
varying types involved.
[*above left*] Champions of the future?
At a show, it is just as important to be
turned out immaculately yourself as it
is for your pony. These pretty girls are
wearing the correct, smart show dress
right down to the attractive button hole,
and their hair is neatly plaited, like their
ponies' manes! Champions are made of
material like this, for if a child is sloppy
he is likely to let his pony go sloppily too
and the combination will be most
unlikely to make the grade of champion.
[*below left*] The phenomenal pony,
Stroller, became a legend in his lifetime.
He is seen here jumping with his owner
Marion Coakes (now Mrs David Mould)
at Hickstead, scene of the British
Jumping Derby, the course for which is
gruelling and includes the famous
Hickstead Derby Bank. Throughout its
14-year history only 15 clear rounds
have been jumped and no less than
three of these have been by the 14.2 h.h.
pony Stroller. He represented Britain
in the Mexico Olympic Games and he
helped his owner to win numerous
prizes and great victories. Every time
he entered an arena great cheers went up
from appreciative crowds. He started in
junior events and when Marion
graduated to senior class she could find
no horse to compare with her pony so
she retained his services, with such
exceptional success, in the adult events.
No wonder that after his retirement in
1973 he was invited as star guest for the
Parade of Personalities at the Horse of
the Year Show. He bowed proudly at
the thunderous applause, but doubtless
wondered where the jumps had got to!

Index

Acknowledgments

The publishers would like to thank the following individuals and organizations for their kind permission to reproduce the pictures in this book:

A. F. A. Colour Library	12
Aspect Picture Library	13 above
Barnaby's Picture Library	25 above
John Carnemolia	55 above, 69 below, 88–89
Bruce Coleman Ltd.	79 below
Anne Cumbers	22 above, 43 above, 48 below, 50 above, 66
Derek Davies	33 above, 62, 76, endpapers
Reginald Davis	90 centre
Robert Estall	8–9 below, 19 below, 21
Expression Photo Library	29
Sonia Halliday	40–41 above
Robert Harding Associates	15 above, 17, 35, 63 above
Ed Lacey	92 above, 93 above, 93 below
Jane Miller	7, 20, 68, 77, 78, 82 below, 84
John Moss	18 above, 36, 37 below, 39 below, 48 above, 49, 50 below, 63 below, 69 below, 71 above, 71 below, 90 above, 94 above
Morris Newcombe	59
Photographic Library of Australia	26 above, 45 above
Pictor Ltd.	14, 22 below, 30 below, 32, 38 below, 44 above, 47, 65, 74, 87
Peter Roberts	54, 61, 95 above, 95 below
Iantha Ruthven	24, 28, 53, 81
John Scott	90 below, 91 above, 91 below
Spectrum Colour Library	2–3, 6, 8 above, 10, 11 above, 16, 23, 25 below, 33 below, 34, 37 above, 38 above, 39 above, 40–41 below, 41 above, 43 below, 44 below, 55 below, 60, 67, 72–73, 75, 80, 82 above
Tony Stone Associates	1, 4–5, 19 above, 42, 56–57, 79 above, 83, front jacket, back jacket
Syndication International Ltd.	45 below, 52, 85, 92 below, 94 below
S. A. Thompson	9 above, 11 below, 13 below, 15 below, 18 below, 26 below, 27, 30 above, 31, 46, 51, 58, 64, 70, 86